THE
Little Book
— OF —
ZEN
WISDOM

THE
Little Book
— OF —
ZEN
WISDOM

Compiled by
John Baldock

ELEMENT
Shaftesbury, Dorset ◆ Rockport, Massachusetts
Brisbane, Queensland

© Element Books Ltd
This compilation © John Baldock 1994

Published in Great Britain in 1994 by
ELEMENT BOOKS LTD
Shaftesbury, Dorset

Published in the USA in 1994 by
ELEMENT, INC.
42 Broadway, Rockport, MA 01966

Published in Australia in 1994 by
ELEMENT BOOKS LTD
for JACARANDA WILEY LTD
33 Park Road, Milton, Brisbane, 4064

Designed and created by:
The Bridgewater Book Company/Ron Bryant-Funnell
Picture research by Felicity Cox
Textual photographs by Sarah Bentley
Printed and bound in Great Britain by:
William Clowes Ltd, Beccles, Suffolk

British Library Cataloguing in Publication data available

Library of Congress Cataloging in Publication data available

ISBN 1-85230-563-0

FOREWORD

The sayings and stories gathered together in these pages offer the reader a small taste of the profound humour and wisdom of Zen masters from across the centuries.

Whatever words or methods he uses – from the traditional *koan* (riddle) and *mondo* (debate) to practical jokes or physical assault – the role of the Zen Master is essentially that of the finger pointing to the moon. In this case the 'moon' is enlightenment or self-realization – the letting go of all physical and mental preconceptions so that reality can be experienced both instantly and directly, as it *is*.

So, whether you choose to dip into these pages at random or read them from cover to cover, give the words of the Zen masters time to roll around your mind so that you can truly savour the taste of Zen. Or, in the words of the sage Lao-Tzu:

Do things *wu-wei*, by doing nothing
Achieve without trying to achieve anything –
Savour the taste of what you cannot taste.

(Where a master is generally known by both the Chinese and Japanese forms of his name, both have been given.)

Everything in the universe comes
out of Nothing.
Nothing – the nameless
is the beginning . . .
Follow the nothingness of the Tao,
and you can be like it, not needing
anything,
seeing the wonder and the root of
everything.

Tao Te Ching: 1

The teaching that leads to transformation is *furyu monji*,★ that is Zen. There is no teacher to ask, nor the chance to be elucidated. There is nothing to teach. This is the method of self-enlightenment. One simply exerts oneself with all one's might towards the state where even one thought does not arise.

Dogen (1200 - 1253)

★ furyu monji *means 'not depending on the written word'. Here it can be translated as 'direct experience'.*

Upon a soul absolutely free
from thoughts and emotions,
Even the tiger finds no room
to insert its fierce claws.

Zen poem

ONE-FINGER ZEN

The Zen master Gutei made a practice of raising his finger whenever he answered a question about Zen. A very young pupil began to imitate him, and whenever any one asked the pupil what his master had been teaching about, the boy would raise his finger.

Gutei got to hear about this, and when he came upon the boy as he was doing it one day, he grabbed hold of him and cut off his finger.

As the boy ran off crying, Gutei shouted, 'Stop!' The boy stopped, turned round, and looked at his Master through his tears.

Gutei was holding up his own finger. The boy went to hold up his finger, and when he realized it wasn't there he bowed to the Master.

In that instant the boy became enlightened.

Zen story

Do not seek to follow in the
footsteps of the Masters; seek
what they sought.

Zen saying

Only when you have no thing in
your mind and no mind in things are
you vacant and spiritual,
empty and marvellous.

Te-shan/Tokusan (780-865)

Stop talking, stop thinking, and there is nothing you will not understand.

Return to the Root and you will find the Meaning;

Pursue the Light, and you will lose its source . . .

There is no need to seek Truth: only stop having views.

Seng-ts'an / Sosan (d. 600)

Four students of Zen promised one another to meditate for seven days in silence.

On the first day all were silent. Their meditation had begun auspiciously, but when night came and the oil-lamps were growing dim one of the students could not help exclaiming to a servant. 'Fix those lamps.'

The second student was surprised to hear the first one talk. 'We are not supposed to say a word,' he remarked.

'You two are stupid. Why did you talk?' asked the third.

'I am the only one who has not talked,' boasted aloud the fourth student.

Zen story

When walking just walk,
When sitting just sit,
Above all, don't wobble.

Yun-men / Ummon (d.949)

NO-MIND, NO-THOUGHT

A monk asked a Zen Master, 'What does one think of while sitting?'†

'One thinks of not-thinking,' the Master replied.

'How does one think of not-thinking?' the monk asked.

'Without thinking,' said the Master.

Zen story

† *'sitting' refers to the practice of za-zen or meditation.*

Many people are afraid to empty their minds lest they may plunge into the Void. They do not know that their own Mind is the Void. The ignorant eschew phenomena but not thought; the wise eschew thought but not phenomena.

Huang-po/Obaku (d. circa 850)

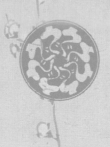

Before a person studies Zen,
mountains are mountains and waters
are waters; after a first insight into the
truth of Zen, mountains are no
longer mountains and waters are not
waters; but after enlightenment,
mountains are once again mountains
and waters are waters.

Ch'ing-yuan/Seigen (d.740)

It is the same and at the same time it
is not the same.
It is different and it is not different.

Zen saying

Those who seek the truth by means of intellect and learning only get further and further away from it. Not till your thoughts cease all their branching here and there, not till you abandon all thoughts of seeking for something, not till your mind is motionless as wood or stone, will you be on the right road to the Gate.

Huang-Po/Obaku (d. circa 850)

Not knowing how near the Truth is,
People seek it far away – what a pity!
They are like him who, in the midst
of water,
Cries in thirst so imploringly.

Hakuin (1683-1768)

✦

EMPTY YOUR CUP

A university professor visited Nan-in to inquire about Zen.

Nan-in served tea. He filled his visitor's cup and then kept on pouring. The professor watched the overflow until he could restrain himself no longer. 'It is overfull. No more will go in.'

'Like this cup,' Nan-in said, 'you are full of your own opinions and speculations. How can I show you Zen unless you first empty your cup?'

Zen story

WASH YOUR BOWL

A monk came to Chao-chou [Joshu] and asked, 'What is the meaning of Zen?'

The Master replied, 'Have you eaten your breakfast?'

'Yes,' said the monk, 'I have eaten.'

'Then wash your bowl,' said Chao-chou.

At that instant the monk was enlightened.

Zen story

People in the world
Do not doubt
It is teaching
Which is the
beginning of doubt.

Zen poem

To learn the way of the
Buddha is to learn about
oneself. To learn about oneself
is to forget oneself. To forget
oneself is to be enlightened by
everything in the world. To be
enlightened by everything in
the world is to let fall one's
own body and mind.

Dogen (1200 - 1253)

One in All.
All in One —
If only this is realized,
No more worry about your
not being perfect!

Seng-ts'an/Sosan (d.600)

Look within, thou *art* Buddha.

Zen saying

WHAT IS BUDDHA?

A monk asked Ma-tsu [Baso]: 'What is Buddha?' Ma-tsu replied: 'This mind is Buddha.'

A monk asked Ma-tsu: 'What is Buddha?' Ma-tsu replied: 'This mind is not Buddha.'

Zen koan

As far as Buddha-nature is
concerned, there is no difference
between an enlightened man and an
ignorant one. What makes the
difference is that the one realizes it,
while the other is kept in ignorance
of it.

Hui-neng/Daikan (637-713)

If anyone regards *bodhi*
[enlightenment] as something to be
attained, to be cultivated by
discipline, he is guilty of the pride
of self.

Saptasatika-prajna-paramita Sutra: 234

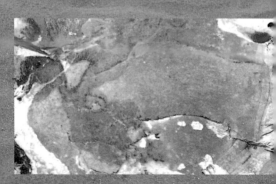

INSIDE OR OUTSIDE
THE MIND?

Fa-yen [Hogen] lived alone in a small temple in the country. One day he overheard four travelling monks arguing about subjectivity and objectivity. He joined them and said: 'There is a big stone. Do you consider it to be inside or outside your mind?'

One of the monks replied: 'From the Buddhist viewpoint everything is an objectification of mind, so I would say that the stone is inside my mind.'

'Your head must feel very heavy, then,' observed Fa-yen, 'if you are carrying around a stone like that in your mind.'

Zen story

ACTION SPEAKS LOUDER
THAN WORDS

Po-chang [Hyakujo] had so many
students that he had to open a new
monastery. To find a suitable person
to appoint as its master, he called his
monks together and set a pitcher of
water in front of them, saying:
'Without calling it a pitcher of water,
tell me what it is.'

The head monk said, 'You
couldn't call it a piece of wood.'

At this the monastery cook kicked
the pitcher over and walked away.
The cook was put in charge of the
new monastery.

Zen story

If you work on your mind with your mind,
How can you avoid an immense confusion?

Seng-ts'an / Sosan (d. 600)

It is the mind itself
which leads the mind astray.
Guard against the mind.

Zen poem

The perfect man employs his mind
as a mirror. It grasps nothing; it
refuses nothing. It receives, but it
does not keep.

Chuang-tzu/Soshi (d. circa 275 BC)

IS THAT SO?

The Zen master Hakuin was honoured by his neighbours as one who led a pure life.

One day it was discovered that a beautiful girl who lived near Hakuin was pregnant. Her parents were very angry. At first the girl would not say who the man was, but after much harassment she named Hakuin.

In great anger the parents went to Hakuin, but all he had to say to them was, 'Is that so?'

After the child was born it was taken to Hakuin, who took very good care of the child, obtaining milk, food, and everything else the child needed from his neighbours.

A year later the girl-mother could stand it no longer, so she told her parents the truth – the real father of the child was a young man who worked in the fish market. The mother and father of the girl at once went to Hakuin to tell him the story, apologize at length, ask his forgiveness, and get the child back again.

Hakuin listened to them and then, as he willingly yielded the child, he said, 'Is that so?'

Zen story

A person may appear a fool and yet
not be one. He may only be guarding
his wisdom carefully.

Zengetsu

WHAT IS IT THAT MOVES?

Two monks were arguing about a flag blowing in the wind.

One said: 'The flag is moving.'

The other said: 'The wind is moving.'

Hui-neng [Daikan], the Sixth Patriarch, happened to be passing by. He told them: 'Not the wind, not the flag; mind is moving.'

In that instant both monks became enlightened.

Zen story

THE WINDOW OF
ENLIGHTENMENT

Enlightenment means seeing through
to your own essential nature and this
at the same time means seeing
through to the essential nature of the
cosmos and all things. For seeing
through to essential nature is the
window of enlightenment. One may
call essential nature truth if one wants
to. In Buddhism from ancient times
it has been called suchness or
Buddha-nature or one Mind. In Zen
it has been called nothingness, the
one hand, or one's original face. The
designations may be different, but the
content is completely the same.

Hakuun Yasutani Roshi (1885-1973)

What is the sound of one hand clapping?

Zen koan

SEEING INTO ONE'S OWN NATURE

If you take up one koan and
investigate it without ceasing, your
thoughts will die and your ego-
demands will be destroyed. It is as
though a vast abyss opened up in
front of you, with no place to put
your hands and feet. You face death,
and your heart feels as though it were
on fire. Then suddenly you are one
with the koan, and body and mind
let go . . . . This is known as seeing
into one's own nature. You must
push forward relentlessly, and with
the help of this great concentration
you will penetrate without fail to the
infinite source of your own nature.

Hakuin (1683-1768)

WHO BINDS YOU?

A pupil asked Seng-ts'an [Sosan]:
'What is the method of liberation?'

'Who binds you?' replied
Seng-ts'an.

'No one binds me.'

'Why then,' asked Seng-ts'an,
'should you seek liberation?'

In that instant the pupil became
enlightened.

Zen story

You cannot describe it,

you cannot picture it.

You cannot admire it,

you cannot feel it.

It is your real self,

which has no hiding-place.

When the world is destroyed,

it will not be destroyed.

Zen poem

NO WORK, NO FOOD

Po-chang [Hyakujo], the Chinese Zen master, used to labour with his pupils even at the age of eighty, trimming the gardens, cleaning the grounds, and pruning the trees.

The pupils felt sorry to see the old teacher working so hard, but they knew he would not listen to their advice to stop, so they hid away his tools.

That day the master did not eat. The next day he did not eat, nor the next. 'He may be angry because we have hidden his tools,' the pupils surmised. 'We had better put them back.'

The day they did, the teacher worked and ate the same as before. In the evening he instructed them: 'No work, no food.'

Zen story

W ithout going anywhere,
      you can know the whole world.
Without even opening your window,
      you can know the ways of Heaven.
You see: the further away you go, the
      less you know . . .

Tao Te Ching: 47

There is no Buddha, no spiritual path to follow, no training and no realization. What are you feverishly running after?

Lin-chi / Rinzai (d.867)

Sitting quietly, doing nothing,
Spring comes, and the grass grows by
itself.

The Zenrin

ACKNOWLEDGEMENTS

Permission to reproduce copyright material has been sought in connection with the following quotations. While every effort has been made to secure permissions, if there are any errors or oversights regarding copyright material, we apologize and will make suitable acknowledgement in any future edition.

Pp. 5, 7, 43: *Tao Te Ching: The New Translation*. Translation copyright ©1993 Man-Ho Kwok, Martin Palmer, Jay Ramsay.

Pp. 30, 31, 40: *The Way of Zen*, Alan Watts. Copyright ©1957 Pantheon Books, a division of Random House, Inc.

Pp. 8, 17b, 22, 32: *Immovable Wisdom – The Art of Zen Strategy: The Teachings of Takuan Soho*. Compiled and translated by Nobuko Hirose. Copyright ©1992 Nobuko Hirose.

Pp. 9, 33, 41: *The Modern Mystic: A New Collection of Early Writings of Alan Watts*. Copyright ©1990 Mark Watts and John Snelling.

P. 13: *Buddhist Texts,* ed. Edward Conze. Bruno Casirer (Publisher), Oxford.

Pp. 14, 20, 26, 29, 35, 36, 42: *Zen Flesh, Zen Bones*. Compiled by Paul Reps. Copyright ©1957 Charles E. Tuttle Co., Inc.

Pp. 15a, 21, 23, 37, 39, 44: *The Elements of Zen*. Copyright ©1992 David Scott and Tony Doubleday.

Pp. 16, 18: *The Zen Teaching of Huang Po*, translated by John Blofeld. Rider, London.

P. 19: *Essays in Zen Buddhism,* by D. T. Suzuki. Rider,

London and Grove Press, Inc., New York.
P. 27: *The Chinese on the Art of Painting,* by Oswald Sirèn. Schocken Books, New York.
P. 45: *Haiku* Vol. 1, ed. R. H. Blyth. The Hokuseido Press.

The publishers would like to thank the following for permission to reproduce their illustrations:
The Bridgeman Art Library – pages 9, 16–17
E.T. Archive, British Museum – pages 10–11, 32–3
E.T. Archive, Freer Gallery of Art – pages 12, 46.

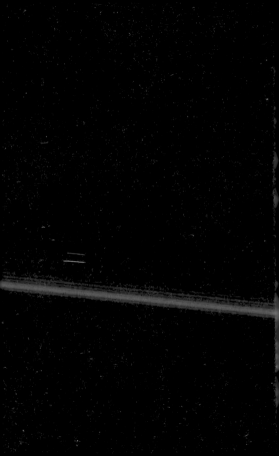